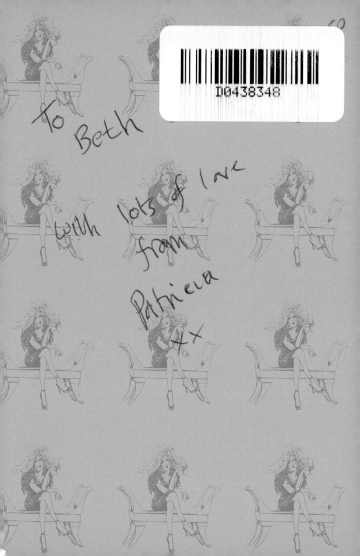

To Beth

with lots of love

from

Patricia

4x

Older, Wiser... Sexier

summersdale

OLDER, WISER... SEXIER

Summersdale Publishers Ltd
46 West Street
Chichester
West Sussex
PO19 1RP
UK

www.summersdale.com

Printed and bound in China

ISBN: 978-1-84953-020-0

Substantial discounts on bulk quantities of Summersdale books are available to corporations, professional associations and other organisations. For details contact Summersdale Publishers by telephone: +44 (0) 1243771107, fax: +44 (0) 1243 786300 or email: nicky@summersdale.com.

Older, Wiser... Sexier

Bev Williams

Age is just a number. It's totally irrelevant unless, of course, you happen to be a bottle of wine.

Joan Collins

I'm like old wine. They don't bring me out very often, but I'm well preserved.

Rose Fitzgerald Kennedy

'I love cooking with wine.

Occasionally I add food.'

I'm not sixty, 'I'm sexty'.

Dolly Parton

Sex appeal is 50 per cent what
you've got and 50 per cent what
people think you've got.

Sophia Loren

Put a sparkle into your relationship
with a little pole –

vaulting.

If they don't have chocolate in heaven I'm not going.

Roseanne Barr

Chocolate, coffee and men –

some things are so much better rich.

I think your whole life shows in your face, and you should be proud of that.

Lauren Bacall

Good cheekbones are the brassiere of old age.

Barbara de Portago

'It's amazing how many of my stray eyebrows –

are now stuck on my chin!'

It's true, some wines improve with age. But only if the grapes were good in the first place.

Abigail Van Buren

Wine is a living liquid containing no preservatives.

Julia Child

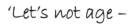

'Let's not age –

Let's just marinate.'

Old age is an excellent time for outrage. My goal is to say or do at least one outrageous thing every week.

Maggie Kuhn

The older one grows, the more one likes indecency.

Virginia Woolf

At your age, people expect you to be
mature, wise and sensible...

disillusion them.

When Sears comes out
with a riding vacuum
cleaner, then I'll clean
the house.

Roseanne Barr

Housework?

Just sweep the room with a glance.

Beautiful young people are
accidents of nature, but beautiful
old people are works of art.

Eleanor Roosevelt

If you survive long enough, you're
revered – rather like an old building.

Katherine Hepburn

All women over 45 are
really goddesses –

and should be worshipped daily.

I got my figure back after giving birth. Sad, I'd hoped to get somebody else's.

Caroline Quentin

We are always the same age inside.

Gertrude Stein

'If God had meant me
to touch my toes –

he would have put
chocolates on the floor.'

Men don't get cellulite. God might just be a man.

Rita Rudner

After thirty, a body has a mind of its own.

Bette Midler

One in five men think cellulite is a battery...

God bless them.

I've never met a woman
in my life who would
give up lunch for sex.

Erma Bombeck

Cooking is like love.

It should be indulged in with abandon.

If you obey all the rules, you miss all the fun.

Katherine Hepburn

The lovely thing about being forty is that you can appreciate twenty-five-year-old men more.

Colleen McCullough

'Just how naughty can we be –

and still go to heaven?'

You can't turn back the clock. But you can wind it up again.

Bonnie Prudden

Fitness – if it came in a bottle, everybody would have a great body.

Cher

The best way to enjoy yourself –

is very, very, very... badly.

When I'm old and grey,
I want to have a house by
the sea. And paint. With
a lot of wonderful chums,
good music and booze
around. And a damn
good kitchen to cook in.

Ava Gardner

When we are happy, we eat, when we are sad, we eat...

when exactly don't we eat?

Our ability to delude ourselves may
be an important survival tool.

Jane Wagner

Time may be a great healer, but it's
a lousy beautician.

Anonymous

'Grey? you call it grey?

It's stress highlights – if you don't mind!'

I have everything I had 20 years ago, only it's all a little bit lower.

Gypsy Rose Lee

Time is a dressmaker specialising in alterations.

Faith Baldwin

'Mirror, mirror on the wall...

I am my mother after all.'

I do wish I could tell you my age but it's impossible. It keeps changing all the time.

Greer Garson

Like many women my age, I am 28 years old.

Mary Schmich

'My husband is quite used to
growing old by himself.

I haven't had a birthday for years!'

Seize the moment. Remember all those women on the *Titanic* who waved off the dessert cart.

Erma Bombeck

My advice if you insist on slimming: eat as much as you like – just don't swallow it.

Harry Secombe

'It's taken a lot of willpower –

but I've finally kicked the urge to diet.

There comes a time in every
woman's life when the only thing
that helps is a glass of champagne.

Bette Davis

Champagne is the only wine that
leaves a woman beautiful after
drinking it.

Madame De Pompadour

'I'm a multi-tasker.

I go to parties, I smile, I talk, I enjoy great food and I have little drinkies.'

I worry about scientists discovering that lettuce has been fattening all along.

Erma Bombeck

As long as a woman's flesh is clean
and healthy what does it matter
what shape she is?

Ian Fleming

I would rather be round and jolly
than thin and cross.

Ann Widdecombe

'I put on another pound this morning.

It must be my new deodorant.'

Birthdays are nature's way of
telling us to eat more cake.

Anonymous

Between two evils, I always pick the
one I never tried before.

Mae West

'It's not fluid retention I'm afraid.

It's cake retention.'

The best way to get a husband to do anything is to suggest he is too old to do it.

Felicity Parker

We learn from experience that men never learn from experience.

George Bernard Shaw

When a man appears sexy, caring
and entertaining –

give him a couple of days and he'll
be back to normal.

I never do any television without chocolate. Quite often I write the scripts and I make sure there are chocolate scenes... It's amazing I'm so slim!

Dawn French

'You would think somebody somewhere could invent a chocolate...

with the calories of celery!'

One of the best parts of growing older? You can flirt all you like since you've become harmless.

Liz Smith

If I'm feeling really wild, I don't floss before bedtime.

Judith Viorst

'I've sinned again.'

Housework can't kill you,
but why take a chance?

Phyllis Diller

'Oh yes, I always keep a few cards around.

People think I've been ill, so I can't clean the house.'

As you get older, the pickings get slimmer, but the people don't.

Carrie Fisher

I never worry about diets. The only carrots that interest me are the number you get in a diamond.

Mae West

Life has got to be lived. That's all
there is to it.

Eleanor Roosevelt

The age of a woman doesn't mean a
thing. The best tunes are played on
the oldest fiddles.

Ralph Waldo Emerson

Just take life with a pinch of salt...

a slice of lime and two
shots of tequila.

If I had my life to live over again, I'd make the same mistakes, only sooner.

Tallulah Bankhead

It's sex, not youth, that's wasted on the young.

Janet Harris

'We only have one regret at our age –

and that's all the sins
we didn't commit.'

I have bursts of being a lady, but it doesn't last long.

Shelley Winters

I mean what's so fulfilling about fulfilment anyway?

Maureen Lipman

Never go jogging.

It makes the ice in your glass jump.

I believe in loyalty; I think when a woman reaches an age she likes she should stick to it.

Eva Gabor

No woman should ever be quite accurate about her age. It looks so calculating.

Oscar Wilde

To be an ageless beauty, all you have to do...

is give up birthdays. And lie about absolutely everything.

Time and trouble will tame an advanced young woman, but an advanced old woman is uncontrollable by any earthly force.

Dorothy L. Sayers

'Take my advice and never drink water.

I've seen what it does to the bottom of boats.'

My doctor told me to do something that puts me out of breath, so I've taken up smoking again.

Jo Brand

I don't plan to grow old gracefully; I plan to have facelifts until my ears meet.

Rita Rudner

No exercise is impossible.

Hopeless maybe – but not
impossible.

You only live once, but if you do it right, once is enough.

Mae West

Good judgement comes from experience, and often experience comes from bad judgement.

Rita Mae Brown

On the whole, the years have been kind to us...

it was just the weekends which got us into trouble.

The easiest way to diminish the appearance of wrinkles is to keep your glasses off when you look in the mirror.

Joan Rivers

Please don't retouch my wrinkles. It took me so long to earn them.

Anna Magnani

Go without a bra –

and pull the wrinkles
out of your face.

Old age is no place for sissies.

Bette Davis

If life throws you a lemon – make
lemonade.

Joan Collins

Life's too short to stuff a
mushroom.

Shirley Conran

The secret of staying young is to
live honestly, eat slowly and lie
about your age.

Lucille Ball

Never eat healthy food...

we so need all the preservatives we
can get.

A woman never forgets
her age – once she decides
what it is.

Stanley Davis

Have you enjoyed this book? If so, why not write a review on your favourite website?

Thanks very much for buying this Summersdale book.